Whales and Dolphins for Kids
Oceans of The World in Color

BABY PROFESSOR
EDUCATION KIDS

Speedy Publishing LLC
40 E. Main St. #1156
Newark, DE 19711
www.speedypublishing.com

Copyright 2018

Dolphins and whales all belong to a group of marine animals known as cetaceans. Cetaceans are warm-blooded, breathe air, and give birth to living offspring and nurse their young.

Whales are the largest animals that have ever lived on earth and are the largest animals that live in the ocean.

There are two types of whales, Baleen Whales and Toothed Whales. Baleen whales use a plate of comb-like fibre called baleen to filter small crustaceans and other creatures from the water.

Whales migrate further than any other animal. Whales migrate to warmer waters. When whales are migrating they can be seen blowing and jumping out of the water, this jumping is called breaching.

Whales are the loudest animals in the world. The sounds they make are called "Whale Song." These underwater sounds can travel great distances.

Dolphins live in schools or pods formed by 10 to 12 individuals. Female dolphins are called cows, males are called bulls and young dolphins are called calves.

Compared to other animals, dolphins are believed to be very intelligent. Dolphins communicate with each other by clicking, whistling and other sounds.

The Killer Whale also known as Orca is a type of dolphin. The killer whale is also the biggest known dolphin.

CPSIA information can be obtained
at www.ICGtesting.com
Printed in the USA
LVHW060850020421
683278LV00026B/158